WaterColourWorld

World poems

Meera Jenkal Bhat

India | USA | UK

Made with ❤ on the BookLeaf Publishing Platform
www.bookleafpub.in
www.bookleafpub.com

Dedication

To my parents and sister.
To all the people who love poetry and a world of
collective consciousness.

Preface

Poetry is the art of capturing fleeting moments, the whispers of emotion, and the colors of the soul. *Water Colour World* is a collection of verses that flow like paint on canvas, blending dreams, memories, and reflections into a landscape of words.

Like watercolors, life is fluid, unpredictable, and beautifully imperfect. Each poem in this book is a brushstroke on the canvas of existence—some delicate and translucent, others bold and intense. These verses explore the gentle ebb and flow of love, the turbulence of loss, the serenity of nature, and the wonder of imagination. They invite you to see the world not just as it is but as it could be—softened at the edges, blurred with feeling, and illuminated by the light of possibility.

Watercolor paintings and poetry share a common truth: they embrace imperfection. A drop of ink spreading across damp paper, just as a thought spills onto the page, is never fully controlled. And yet, in that surrender, beauty is born. This book is an invitation to embrace that beauty—the half-formed ideas, the emotions that bleed into one another, and the images that emerge from the unexpected.

Whether you find solace in the quiet hues of dawn, the stormy grays of sorrow, or the golden glow of hope, *Water Colour World* is a journey through shades of feeling and imagination. Each poem is a window into a different world, a different mood, a different story.

Let these pages wash over you like watercolor on paper, blurring the lines between reality and reverie. May you find in them something of yourself—reflected, refracted, and rendered in shades of poetry.

Love,
Meera Jenkal Bhat

Acknowledgements

Thank you to Bookleaf Publishing for creating this wonderful opportunity. And thank you in advance to all the readers out there.

1. A child of the Universe

When birds sing.
I sing with them.
When butterflies fly.
I fly with them.
I whisper to the winds.
I dance under the skies.
I find rhythm to the river.
And float to the ocean.
To the One.
In devotion.
A child of the universe am I.
A miracle in my eye.

Thy light always shining on me.
I am free.

When the starts twinkle.
I twinkle with them.
When Angels visit.
I visit places with them.

I tell stories to the moon.
I keep a light on for dreams.
I pray to God.
I save Hope for tomorrow.
And swallow sorrow.
Give happiness out for borrow.
A child of the universe am I.
A miracle in my eye.
A child of the universe am I.
A miracle in my eye.

Thy light always shining on me.
I am free.

19.05.2023

2. A love beyond labels

Business icon or stay-at-home mom.
In a relationship or single.
Messy bun or sleek hairdo.
Comfy PJs or cocktail dress.
You can be all.
You can be none.
How dare anyone define.
If you are living life full and fun.

In a world where everything flows and lulls.
Maybe all that is needed is a love beyond labels.

Sporty strong or nerdy geek.
Party person or home bound.
Flat abs or mushroom tops.
Traditional soul or modern rebel.
You can be all.
You can be none.
How dare anyone define.
If you are living life full and fun.

In a world where everything flows and lulls.
Maybe all that is needed is a love beyond labels.
Halos and skulls.
A love beyond labels.

12.02.2021

3. A simple song

I don't have much.
But I'll easily share.
My heart is in sorrow.
But I'll gladly care.
I am kind of lonely.
But if you need help, I'll be there.
I am often silent.
But I have words of kindness to spare.

Ooooooo. Ooooooo.
I'm trying to be true.
Ooooooo. Ooooooo.
I'm trying to reach You.

I wear a mask.
But my soul is bare.
I do feel suffocated.
But I'll ask you if you need air.
I sometimes feel timid.
But I'll lend you courage to dare.

I've lost many dreams.
But I'll save you from your nightmare.

Ooooooo. Ooooooo.
I'm trying to be true.
Ooooooo. Ooooooo.
I'm trying to reach You.

Ooooooo. Ooooooo.
Ooooooo. Ooooooo.
Ooooooo. Ooooooo.

12.6.2020

4. A song for everyone

Why don't you go sit under the sun?
Why not have some fun.
Leave aside the world-weary worry.
Life as it is passes by in a hurry.

Sing a song for everyone.
Sing to the One.
Let Angels hear you.
And make all your wishes come true.

Why don't you go sit under the trees?
And look for fairies no one sees.
Watch dew drops glisten on the grass.
Find solitude away from the people mass.

Why don't you go sit under the moon?
And do a liberating wolf croon.
Leave behind the day's burdens.
And think of the innocence that was once.

Sing a song for everyone.
Sing to the One.
Let Angels hear you.
And make all your wishes come true.

26.02.2020

5. A tale about a tail

On a sunny day, they laid him to rest.
She held his collar against her chest.
They said he'd gone away. Oh! forever.
But she did not cry, she was far too clever.

They did not know that she knew better.
About a land called Heaven, where all got together.
A land of strawberries and chocolate milk.
Where angels flew and walked on silk.

She knew he'd be happy there, but she missed him so!
He couldn't come back, so she decided to go.
There was a road to Heaven, where the sun set.
She wore her best clothes 'n took food in a basket.

Her little legs carried her. On and on.
Road to road. Night and dawn.
Even when the pain came, in a little red drop.
She struggled on and didn't stop.

When she couldn't move, on the grass she laid.
She had to find him. So she prayed.
Her eyes closed, the world grew dim.
When she woke up, she had found Him.

13.10.2016

6. A thousand thoughts a day

A thousand thoughts a day.
Can go away when you pray.
Just a moment of silence.
Just a moment of stillness.
Just a moment of inner sense.
Just a moment of lightness.
At first it is not easy.
It's a mix of fear and fidgety.
But if you go at it with continuity.
Maybe you will discover divinity.
A thousand thoughts a day.
Can go away when you pray.
And eventually all will be okay.

23.02.2021

7. A toast to friendship

Let us be together, always forever;
Let our ways never part.
Our ups & downs to share together,
Memories close to our heart.
People come only to go,
But let us not be one of them.
Of our strength let them know,
When they choose to condemn.
Even though we may be far apart,
Our thoughts will bring us near.
A promise we hold in our heart,
Of closeness through the years.
If we do lose each other,
In heaven will cross our ways.
Our immortal souls then locked together,
This time for eternity; for always.

2.08.2016

8. A whole universe inside of me

There's a whole universe inside of me.
It's just a little bit dark now.
All it will take is a little bit of self-love.
To be that spirited spark again.
No negative noises.
My own choices.
Hopes, dreams, and inspired inner voices.
There's a whole universe inside of me.
Waiting to be set free.

6.4.2022

9. About giving

When I see others suffer.
I feel a pain in my heart.
But I am in no position to help everyone.
So I try to do what I can.
But often that doesn't feel enough.
And sometimes I can be selfish.
And gratify my own needs.
Then I feel sad after.
Like why couldn't I spare.
What I can't do in need I try for in words.
Like a kind word or a kind thought.
Sometimes I aim for poet Rumi's words.
Once I thought I was so smart that I could change the
world.
But now I'm trying to be wise and change myself.

23.05.2023

10. Adulting

Sometimes I know my life is falling apart.
So I put my troubles on a cart.
And push it down a hill.
Worries. Troubles and burdensome a bill.
Thing is I'm now an adult.
Forced to be a part of the capitalism cult.
Drink your coffee and go to work.
No time for a responsibility shirk.
Just when I think I've got a break.
I need to rest my back ache.
I look at pictures old in nostalgia.
And my 90s party pack of memorabilia.
I grew up in times pre technology.
Of cassettes, swings and books of story.
Most people I know have babies already.
While I laugh at memes hysterically.
Sure, it's fun that I get to travel as I please.
But when I walk too fast, I can fall on my knees.
My weekends are spent spread out on bed.
Too much noise can explode my head.

If I eat junk food with a woohoo.
My belly gets broken and bellows blue.
My current metabolism is a riddle or a joke.
Just when I relax a new thought will poke.
Adulting is kinda funny when you think about it.
Life teaches you wisdom and gives you grit.
For sure it is hectic but I'm in for the ride.
After all it's one life to live before I've died.

04.04.2022

11. Afterlife

What is death?
The mere end of breath?
Or is it liberation from this physical trapping?
As we turn into an Angel wing.
And fly into a higher Heaven.
Into a divine Eden.
Where light is there to greet us.
As we board the bliss bus.
Old friends and family surround.
We get to introspect why we were earth bound.
Our soul enjoys the free galaxies.
It's a place of no miseries.
There are so many divine beings.
And serene sights for our seeings.
We bide our time till we may need to return.
And our life lessons once again learn.
With a promise to ease this world's strife.
After what we experienced in our afterlife.

28.02.2020

12. Air-o-space

I want to be free and fly.
Oh let me try.
Oh let me try.
I want to reach the sky.
Oh get me high.
Oh get me high.

In between heavens and hell.
Responding to the blues and bells.
Harmonizing with the universe about what it tells.
In contention with it about what it sells.
Shuffling dreams fantastic or materialistic.
Ruffling winds with a candle on the wick.
In constant cosmic conversations.
Mulling over desires and decisions.

I want to curl up and cry.
Oh I wonder why.
Oh I wonder why.
I want the past to get by.

Oh I wish and sigh.
Oh I wish and sigh.

Maybe then He will see me.
As his girl and give me glory.
Lifting myself from chosen choices.
Shifting personalities with wind voices.
Dealing with supernatural and spiritualistic.
Healing within to relive in miracles and magic;
People echoing my thoughts and words.
Disciple to nature's whims and wonder birds.

I want my third eye.
Oh give me my.
Oh give me my.
I want His reply.
Oh when will I?
Oh when will I?

20.05.2020

13. Anecdotes of a poet's inhabitation

There's a man who sits across the street.
Saving a smile for everyone he does meet.
Painting a world that no one sees.
Telling children fascinating stories.
He whistles a merry tune.
Some call him a dreamer, some a loon.
I know him none too well or long.
But when he whistles, I sing along.

There's a dog who believes,
She can see ghosts and fairies.
She hangs her tongue to test the breeze.
As she wanders through gardens and cemeteries.
When others leave, she'll stay.
Guiding spirits who've lost their way.
She may not have a collar or pedigree.
Like the biscuits I give her, she is free.

There is a girl who found Neverland.

When she talks, she does with her hand.
She has friends no one has seen.
And goes places no one has been.
She runs behind glow-worms and butterflies.
Chasing clouds in the skies.
There is a kingdom where she is Queen.
I may not understand, but I know what she means.

There is a frog who lives on a lily.
Croaking a story seemingly silly.
He believes he is a prince.
Cursed by a wizard and a frog ever since.
He sits by the pond and sings every night.
For a love that will change his plight.
If a kiss is all it takes for his dream come true,
Is he so different from me and you?

There is a man who lives by the sea.
People say he doesn't know reality.
He writes letters of love and longing.
A message in a bottle sealed with a ring.
Ever so often, he sails it into oceans deep.
Knowing a mermaid will find it and keep.
As he waits for a fin and harp.
I bring him papers and pencils sharp.

Then there is me who writes poetry.

Wishing of things, as wishes were meant to be.
I make up words, tales and mysteries.
Of people, places and memories.
I spin a world of dreamers and dreams
Where nothing is as it seems.
Who is to say what is true.
Unless it happens to you.

13.10.2016

14. Angry words

Sometimes the things you can say.
Can hurt someone.
And never again make it okay.
And even an apology can't make it better.
Because the damage is already done.
Even if you regret every letter.
Every word has a power behind it.
So be cautious how you use them.
It can heart break or make it lit.
Think before you speak.
Even if in the heat of the moment.
Don't let anger make your word weak.
If this has happened to you.
Learn and never again repeat.
For all you know your foolish words could come true.

26.02.2020

15. Boomerang

Mother!
You would sing a song-
"No matter how long
Time would undo all the wrong."
I have been so good
Know that if I would
I will get what I should
But people have been unkind
They take all they can find
And I am the one left behind
O Mother! When will time turn?
When will they learn?
When will the boomerang return?

For every smile there is a tear.
For every thought there is a fear
For every near there is a far

For every mend there is a scar.

Mother!
They have been winning
While I have been losing
I have doubts in what I am choosing
I ask bad for no one
Just want a sign of reason
Look, yet I find none
How much do I have to wait?
How much more to tolerate?
Is it early; is it too late?
O mother maybe time did turn
Maybe I am to learn
Maybe my boomerang did return

For every wrong there is a right
For every dark there is a light
For every low there is a high
For every welcome there is goodbye

Mother!
You would sing a song
No matter how long
Time would undo all wrong

It didn't happen soon
But I hummed your tune
And found my fortune
Now my name is hallowed
By ample I am followed
I have received what I was owed
O Mother! Time did turn
They all did learn
That every boomerang does return

15.06.2016

16. Bubblewrap

I'm running away...
Leaving everything as is.
Giving my troubles a miss.
I can hear them say-
It's avoidance. It's escapism.
I know they too secretly want to come.
But a capitalist culture conditions to obey.

I'm going away...
Taking a vacation from myself.
Leaving self-help on the bookshelf.
To think only of today-
It's unreality. It's irresponsibility.
Madness belying maturity.
Inner child, come out and play.

I'm floating away...
A particle drifting through space.
Trying to find my own pace.
A place to belong and stay-

It's unwinding. It's undoing.
Logic left at a land lost.
The price somehow worth the cost.

I'm riding away...
Seeking my shining sun.
At a happy hued horizon.
I can hear them pray-
It's a blessing. It's a spell.
An open road my spirit summons.

20.06.2016

17. Chameleon Queen

I'm the magic of a magician.
I'm the ray of the shining sun.
I'm the crescent of the silver moon.
I'm the wisdom of a loon.
I'm the first wink of sleep.
I'm the secrets that you keep.
I'm the end of the rainbow.
Who am I?
Do you know?
Do you know?
I'm the chameleon queen.
Know what I mean.

I'm the smile behind your tear.
I'm the fun behind your fear.
I'm the twists in a fortuitous fate.
I'm the clock that is never late.
I'm the spoke on the wheel of time.
I'm the words of a mime.

I'm the friend in every foe.
Who am I?
Do you know?
Do you know?
I'm the chameleon queen.
Know what I've seen.

I'm the spark before the flame.
I'm the cheating in a game.
I'm the rhythm in a song.
I'm the right in every wrong.
I'm the scent of a flower.
I'm the twenty-fifth hour.
I'm the white of the snow.
Who am I?
Do you know?
Do you know?
I'm the chameleon queen.
Know what I mean.

24.05.2023

18. Chasing clouds

I don't quite know.
Why we're here;
Or where we go.
You and I.
Lost in time.
Finding time.
We will wild.
Chasing clouds. Chasing dreams.
Reach the silver summer sky.
And go searching for stars.

Let's lie down.
And feel the rain.
Kiss the ground.
No one's here.
Nothing's here.
There is all here.
We will smell flowers.
Blow kisses at the moon.
Follow fireflies to a garden.

And go looking for elves.

I will look into your eyes.
And see my world.
You will look into my heart.
And see your life.
We will reach the end.
Of the rainbow.
And paint the sky.
Sit at the edge of the world.
And watch the sun rise.

4.10.2016

19. Choices

Was it my choice how I was born?
I'd like to think yes.
Know of prayer; did it almost every morn.
So I could find His bless.
Think its important to know one's own mind.
In a life full of choices.
It's good to hear your good angel voices.
Although thoughts from the mischief makers in also
needed.
Especially when your inner child needs to be heeded.
Every choice made has an effect.
So, make it well and have your and His protect.
You can govern which way you choose to go.
Even though you don't always know.
Let wisdom and your heart be your guide.
When you don't know which rule to abide.
Try your best to be good and kind.
Try your best to discern your own mind.
Try to win over everybody with love.
And choose to believe that there is a God above.

Watching over.

Helping you start over.

Giving you His love and power.

Still, was it my choice how I was born?

I'd like to think yes.

Know of prayer; did it almost every morn.

So I could find His bless.

That is a choice I choose to make.

For my and His sake.

30.5.2023

20. Circles

I got dismissed from every world I ever knew.
Everyone's egos and horns grew.
Unwanted everywhere.
I acted like I did not care.
A lot of times I was not there.
I knew I wanted to belong.
But no one understood the beat of my heart song.
So, I learnt to sing alone.
Became my own light shone.
And created a wunder world all of my own.

35.03.2023

21. Counting stars. Counting sheep.

Counting stars. Counting sheep.
Where do people go when they sleep?
What is the truth that lies in a dreamer's dream?
You don't realize how precious dreams can be.
Until you don't dream for a while.
It is a channel which sets you free.
To connect with a greater world.
With a greater mind.
In the comfort of pillow curled.
That is the beauty in which God designed.
The concept of dreams.
So, you can alter some fates assigned.
With inspiration.
With imagination.
With ingenuity.
With intellect.
Counting stars. Counting sheep.
Where do people go when they sleep?
I'd like to believe they visit other worlds.

Or maybe others visit them.
I'd like to believe the mind goes on a vacation.
I'd like to believe the brain chews on the day's decision.
I'd like to believe the heart goes into shut down.
Because it too needs a cocoon crown.
Counting stars. Counting sheep.
Never let go of your dreams.
For the price may end up steep.

12.05.2023

22. Cupid is sick

Cupid is sick.

He needs some magic music.

To ignite his fantasy.

And set love free.

What happened is this.

He watched the last of true love's kiss.

In our modern day mayhem.

It became a power struggle between us and them.

People stopped putting in effort.

And cursed cupid which really hurt.

Still he took his arrow and bow.

And sought love high and low.

Over time it became a rare find.

People with romance on their mind.

Not many read a fairy tale.

Or did a God hail.

Still cupid wanted to gift a happy story.

TO people seeking love as their destiny.

His gift was usually made worse.

And the blessing turned into a curse.

Cupid fell in sadness and despair.
That people did not seem to care.
That's why cupid fell sick.
And is in need of magic music.
The kind that our souls sing.
That can soon power his wing.

16.03.2020

23. Curiosity

Some are the places one must not foray.
Some are the things one must not attempt.
So I have been warned.
Admonished even.
But I am peace-less without knowing.
Intrigue driving my fascination.
To seek treacherous territories.
The unwelcome guest.
The persistent pest.
It is both learning and satisfaction I pursue.
In the want to experience all.
In the discerning of secrets.
Not that answers will rest my restless soul.
For further queries will take its place.
Perhaps this tragic flaw, shall lead to my tragedy.
So be it, as long as it comforts my curiosity.

04.10.2016

24. Dare to dream

How good are day dreams?
When nothing happens like it seems.
Don't give up hope I self say.
Let God find me a way I pray.
But sometimes it is hard to hold on.
To dreams big tat float away at dawn.
Then I'm in the world's busyness.
My light embering in its darkness.
I'm an adult with responsibilities.
And no time for wonder whimsies.
Still a what if crosses my mind.
When I a sole second find.
What if my day dreams could come true?
And I could live a life brand new.
What if a star heard me this second?
And its wishes did lend.
What if He is showing me a path?
In spite of my failure aftermath.
That's why I still dare to dream.
How else will I find the magic moon beam.

That will shine its light on me.
And power my success story.

17.10.2019

25. Dawn diary

Dawn is about to break;
And I am still high from last night.
Singing with the birds;
Everything feels alright.

I am standing in between time;
Yesterday still fading.
Tomorrow yet to come.
Who knows what it shall bring.

My feet dance to an inner tune.
Happiness is a melody.
If I hold on to that smile.
Sadness will not follow me.

The world is calm quiet.
It is a soul lifting silence.
A sleepsphere about to wake.
And everything done is past tense.

My eyes watch the horizon new.
A hue of golden glow.
I marvel at the morning muse.
And pray for paradises to flow.

19.05.2020

26. Decisions

We can never tell where a decision will take us.
Never know the precise moment we make it.
But decide...we should.
Then wait to see if we grow up to our decisions.
Or they to us.
There is a beauty in not knowing before.
In one choice lies change.
A whole life rearrange.
An irrevocable shift.
Which could shape our fall or our lift.
Why do we decide what we do?
And how?
Is it guided by emotions or reasoning?
Circumstances or choices?
Or is it made of a moment of clarity.
A certainty beyond duality.
What was the directive of my decision?
Blessing or burden?
I still can't decide.

12.06.2022

27. Dreams

I knocked dream's door.
And asked for Her name.
She said it was all I believed.
All I seek and what I want.
Floating in a cloud of hope.
In dreams I am nothing.
I am all.

I can fly.
I can walk into Heaven.
In dreams, I can dream.

Is it a sign of things to come?
Is it a word of wisdom?
"Why do I dream?"- I asked Her.
She said God has things to say,
For everything you wish and pray.
You may not believe Him.
But dreams you will.

The places I see are new.
The feelings I feel are strange.
Yet I know it from somewhere before.
Is it a part of what I was?
Is it a part of what I will be?
Does it all belong within?
Inside of me.

I am hope.
I am the bearer of faith.
In dreams, I am the dream.

I smush the pillow.
And spread the sheets.
And look toward the starry sky.
In the night's darkness,
I know a light will shine on me.
I free my mind.
And close my eyes.
To see what dreams arise.

19.10.2016

28. Early

Why do people wake up so early in the morning.
When they can go to a land of dreams.
Take a break from reality in a place where nothing is as
it seems.
Sing with the stars and surf on moon beams.

10.02.2022

29. Elysium

There is a restlessness in my soul.
My heart races out of control.
Limited I am by a world of conformity.
Where do I go to set my soul free?
I close my eyes and meditate.
Before I talk, I hesitate.
I feel like I don't quite belong.
I will be gone before long.
For what am I making all this effort?
If you're genuine you get hurt.
Can someone define to me success?
I'd much rather choose happiness.
We're all hurtling to somewhere.
We stomp on who we don't care.
Is this why I was earth bound?
To be a rat racing this ground?
I'm certain my purpose is more.
Like to find that divine door.
Open it and free human kind.
Leave the ugliness behind.

There is a restlessness in my soul.
I wonder who will help make it whole?
I wonder where others like me I'll find.
So we can live with a oneness mind.
We are a divine race.
Let's make this world a paradise place.
You are a divine face.
Let's make this earth a paradise place.

17.10.2019

30. Far near

I wish I could soar with the clouds to the stars.
I wish I could take on any superhuman powers.
And sing all along, losing time, gaining hours.
But I'm here.
The day is clear.
And the world is so far, so near.

I wish I could draw with my feet in the sand.
I wish I could catch rain in my hand.
And reach the edge of the world and stand.
But I'm here.
holding onto fear.
And the world is so far, so near.

I wish I could be the colours of a butterfly.
I wish I could be the sunny rays from the sky.
But I'm here and until I try.
The world will be so far. So near.

So I pack my confidence and sense.

In a bag of experience.
Lose my fright to travel light.
and make my own discovery.
I don't wish to know the way.
I don't wish to leave right now, today.
I wish to make it someday.
Now I'm here.
And it's so dear.
And the world is so near. So far.

04.04.2016

31. Farewell café

I guess this is goodbye.
I don't even want to cry.
We are way past done.
Now I'm on the run.
Into tomorrows.
God knows.
I have to write many stories.
Thank you for all the memories.
But it's time we went our separate ways.
Like seasons on different days.
If walls could talk.
There won't be enough hours on the clock.
We've been happy together.
But we have outgrown each other.
I wish you well.
AS I wish you farewell.
Be good. Do good.
Be how I once understood.
I wish you all the best.
For everything in life and the rest.

You're just a place not a person.
But know that you will always be part of my sun.

05.12.2019

32. Feels like the colour Blue

You may be true,
I bring it on you.
But I'm the one feeling,
like the colour blue.
I've done more than I can deal with.
I can run away.
But where do I go to,
Everything is the colour blue...

What can I do?
Who can I sue?
For painting it all to feel,
like the colour blue.
It maybe that it's genetic,
Or just me sick.
Whatever...perhaps true.
Still, my blood is blue.

I am an artist.
In a blue mist.

And it shows every time,
I flex my wrist.
And every portrait makes me wonder,
If I am her.
I need something new,
That doesn't make me feel blue...

The sky is blue.
Thus the ocean is too.
So, how can I escape feeling,
like the colour blue
If I reach Heaven or Hell,
and ring the bell;
And God too turns out blue.
Then what do I do?
Well, what do I do?

16.10.2016

33. Flying

Flying

I have let go of space as I plunge into bliss.
Soaring in timelessness to a place far beyond.
The world smothering me cannot make me stay.
As I'm flying, I sense no bounds.
The final laughter resounds.
Floating in a passage.
Broken from my cage.
A free spirit light as air.
Belonging somewhere...in the end.
I will fly with the wind and clouds in the sky.
Elevated to a place where all is surreal.
The stars begin to fade, I wave them goodbye.
As I'm flying fear dims.
Angels whisper hymns.
Between heaven and earth.
New found is my worth.
As I'm flying to release.
I have made my peace...in the end.

12.06.2016

34. Fool's Paradise

He walks the ground but sees the skies.
They think him young and none too wise.
Just a fool looking for paradise.
Paradise, the deception of our eyes.
But what if it really lies.
Hidden. A mocking surprise.

Its easy for fools to find paradise.
They don't have wisdom clouding their eyes.
Wisdom that says- all there is, is this.
Stealing children from ignorant bliss.
They grow older, young men so cynical.
Knowledge making them egotistical.
And they laugh at the foolish children.
Dancing in the sun.
They have grown so very wise.
They have lost fools paradise...

An old man walks his worries.
He now knows how time scurries.

Wealth in stealth, piles 'o property
He cant take it with him, can he?
Now he wonders why he spent his lifetime.
Fretting over a dime.
He'd thought a dreamer to be a fool.
But wasn't he the fool who lost his dreams.
In his silent cries.
He waits for fools paradise.

Paradise. In our mind it lies.
A hope, a dream, a priceless prize.
When the child within us dies.
We have killed fool's paradise.
And we wait until our soul dies.

06.10.2016

35. For everyday

For Everyday.
I will say...
Let there be a better tomorrow.
But what we have is enough for today.
What may not or may...
Come our way;
Is not for us to say.
A little hope.
A little pray.
Can make your troubles go away.
And make a deepest wish stay.

For Everyday.
I will say...
Leave a bitter past behind.
Don't pay a heavy price that didn't need a pay.
The light of a new day.
Shone a path.
Hidden below Heaven's ray.
A little dream.

A little pray.
Will ensure you cannot stray.
Find it within you to find the way.

For Everyday.
I will say…
Some things go. Some things come.
Only some things are meant to stay.
One fine day.
Old and grey.
I will still say.
A little smile.
A little faith.
A little pray.
There is no tomorrow like today.

15.06.2022

36. Here

Green grass is wet with dawn's shower.
The sky is on earth, flowing with the river.
The crickets hum to the brook's song.
As I lie in my bed of fresh flowers.
Strumming my guitar, I am a poet.
Staying forever, here...

My feet in the sea, I taste salty winds.
With the waves crashing their welcome.
Digging for snails and shells with my toes.
I wander into my watery crib.
Diving deeper, I am a mermaid.
Unravelling mysteries, here...

There is silence at the edge of a cliff.
Gravity pulls down, the air pulls higher.
Still as the rocks upon which I stand,
I watch the earth sparkle like stars.
Rapt in my senses, I am a hermit.
A meditating soul, here...

The past whispers in ruins standing.
Wild creepers chain down the walls.
As I roam into rooms that once existed,
I sense their lives in me.
Using imagination, I am the queen.
Bestowed with powers, here...

Heaven doesn't seem so far away,
When gazing at the stars and moon.
Spying constellations with my names.
The universe is given another meaning.
Without arithmetic, I am an astronomer.
Creating my own space, here...

Born into something called life.
Made up of what one makes of it.
Searching for the end,
I keep moments dear with me.
Here alone I can't figure.
Who am I? Here...

13.09.2016

37. HocusPocusFocus

Listen to me.
I will show you the world you want to see.
Mistress of magic;
I will show you a world so hypnotic.
In my vision, you are my creation.
I smell your fear;
But curiosity still holds you here.
Stay my friend.
Let us know our mindsend.

That which cannot be understood is feared.
Or given a meaning and revered.
The mind wants to be understood.
It is a beast trained to be good.
The mind is your own travesty.
Changing what you see to what you want to see.
I can liberate you from all that is bleak.
I am the mindfreak.
And oh! The mind is far too clever.
Be careful, or it won't return ever.

Then you will live under its command;
A rabbit, a dove under its wand.
I have the key to a mind's undoing.
I can capture it, before it does your being.
I can call you back from the weak.
I am the mindfreak.
I weave a web of connotation.
A different truth, not imitation.
I will make you little dreams with brandishes of my
wand.
It will fill your mind like grains of sand.
I can read your mind; I can feel your thoughts.
It comes to me in constellations and dots.
I know your words before you speak,
I am the mindfreak.
You don't know the tricks I can conjure.
I can wound, I can cure.
I can tiptoe into your buried secrets.
I can make remember what your mind forgets.
You live life as your mind perceives.
I can change all its beliefs.
I am what you all seek.
I am the mindfreak.

Listen to me.
I will not prey on your vulnerability.
Mistress of mystery;

I am here to set you free.
Teller of tales.
I will make oceans for ships to sail.
And when my work is done here;
Smoke and stars - I disappear.

15.10.2016

38. Hourglass

The grass is higher. The bricks unfamiliar.
A stranger behind the door.
A rusty thing. The rickety swing.
They are here no more.
Just when I think I have gotten it wrong;
A blue bird sings the same old song.
I see the wall I jumped to find freedom;
And the road I took to come back home.

Gone is the field. Left is the lake.
By which I had my first kiss.
City lamps, park benches and satellite towers;
Have taken place of this.
Standing still in good measure,
Is the tree where we buried our treasure.
With the same sun shining above,
I see two people in the same shade of love.

A different sign hangs on a familiar door.

Wormhole windows; in them I see my friends from
before.
Simpler times with hours of talk and hope.
Debate and wait; a wonder kaleidoscope.
The town has changed as I have grown,
But to me, it is still my own.

It's taken years to return and now I have to leave.
I look about; there is happiness as I grieve.
Memories fly with the breeze around.
I lift some sand from the ground.
It will keep in my hourglass.
And let me know of times that pass.

16.10.2016

39. Houses

From the earth arose a tower.
An abode to humble ants.
Partially hidden in garden.
Amid the flowers and plants.

A plant grew into a tree.
For many a year it stood.
Its branches to birds a nest of safety.
Of strong and sturdy wood.

Using little wood a house was built.
After ages of blueprints and overseeing.
A place of dreams and happiness.
A residence for my being.

My being is more than flesh and skin.
A design that leaves me awed.
It is meant to be home to my soul.
So says its architect - God.

Does God reside in the big blue sky?
Watching humans through loss and birth?
Or does He dwell amongst us.
In His house called Earth.

13.09.2018

40. Hugs

I've not been hugged in years.
As the tears,
Stream down my face.
Sometimes I wish I could find a friendly place.
So, I curl up in bed.
And dream of beautiful things.
There's a space in my head.
No one can ever reach.
And I can reach it with wunder wings.

I've not been hugged in years.
As the fears,
Pound my heart.
Sometimes I wish I could find a fresh start.
So, I curl up in bed.
And dream of beautiful things.
There's a space in my head.
No one can ever reach.
And I can reach it with wunder wings.

I've not been hugged in years.
As the seers,
Gather around me.
I feel like a light of love anew.
So, I curl up in bed.
And dream of beautiful things.
There's a space in my head.
I can reach with wunder wings.
And send out hugs for those who need it too.

20.02.2021

41. Human & Divine

God, you say be divine.
And that is perfectly fine.
You say change and cause it.
Pray tell me where do I fit?

Let me explain to you the human side.
Or at least how I feel inside.
How does one settle this divide.
Where does one go to hide.

It's hard to be divine in a world of capitalism.
Have to hold on to hopes and dreams in realism.
I love the girl of idealism.
But the world can sometimes create dualism.

A key, I think, is to hold God in your heart.
And the doing devil in your mind start.
So, you and see and be the change and cause it.
Find the path where destiny, purpose and you fit.

You belong in this world.
And the other.
Don't try to pick and side.
Don't worry or bother.
All the worlds are yours to be in.
As long as you think of them with love from within.

30.5.2023

42. I am what I am

I am my father.
I am my mother.
I am my sister.
I am my lover.
I am thus flying to be a true believer.
I am the creator's verse.
I am true hope's purse.
I am nature's nurse.
I am the poet's verse.
I am thus trying to be a ray receiver.
I am soul sacrifice.
I am eternal eyes.
I am wisdom's wise.
I am thus crying so we may rise.

24.7.2015

43. Illusionary

I linger at the foyer.
Of an orb where twinkling stars are at my realm.
Here I belong.
Where dreams are not fantasy.
The voices in my head not imaginary.
Let me stay...
In my realm of flitting shadow.
The clouds form faces as they fly.
I climb my way onto the rainbow.
And fall with the rain from the sky.
I am not hiding.
Just am a recluse making merry in my delusion.
Needing silence.
Preferring confinement in unreality.
To the truth smothering the sense in me.
Let me stay...
In my realm of golden sundown.
The breeze humming a lullaby.
A queen with roses in her crown.
Falling asleep eternally.

30.05.2016

44. In the mood I was born into

Often, I wear masks.
Head down, completing tasks.
Playing the role people make for me.
I am someone for everybody.

But sometimes I find myself put on the shining shoe.
And dance in the mood I was born into.
Sometimes I am not even a who.
Just an energy in the mood I was born into.

I live in a world beautiful.
Wonder there in colossal and trivial.
How little or big am I?
Related to things beyond the sky.

I am more than meets the eye.
Grounded, my soul is always fly.
Thinking about a Light revolution.
And a spiritual evolution.

I find myself put on the shining shoe.
And dance in the mood I was born into.
Sometimes I am not even a who.
Just an energy in the mood I was born into.

I find myself put on the shining shoe.
And dance in the mood I was born into.
Sometimes I am not even a who.
Just an energy in the mood I was born into.
Pure and pristine.
Cosmic and clean.
Glowing the God gene.
The quintessential queen.

06.10.2020

45. Innergriti

What does it take?
To dream with your eyes open?
To soar without wings or wind.
To stop time with your thoughts.
What does it take?
To make the hard choice easily.
To face challenges without fear.
Or to fear but face them anyway.
To smile in the face of complexity.
And lend a simple solution.
To take the higher road.
And see Heaven.
What does it take?
To find your voice with one word.
To understand that to be understood;
You need to listen.
What does it take?
To begin not knowing the end.
To have patience and wait.
To know your value;

Because you have earned it.
To learn from every mistake.
And even with a loss behind you;
To believe in winning.
What does it take?

16.10.2016

46. It's just

It's just a song.
It's not wrong.
It's simply a song.
To find where I belong.
While playing ping pong.
And get along.

It's just a thought.
It's no ponderous plot.
It's simply a thought.
To find a constellation from my dot.
The wishes I've sought.
It's all I've got.

It's just a word.
That co-occurred.
It's simply a word.
To find my inner bird.
Fly away from untoward.
And feel heard.

It's just a hope.
That helps me cope.
It's simply a hope.
To find free from the mope..
Cut clear from all the dope
Its chances I grope.

It's just a smile.
It's been a while.
It's simply a smile.
To find strength for the mile.
Run beyond the problems pile.
And do it in style.

7.3.2016

47. Life lessons

Witty clauses.
And practised pauses.
Are the ways of working society.
But it is not always who one should be.

Not all of them are your friends.
You have to judge whom He sends.
And when you wonder how you chose.
Your heart always knows.

Don't believe in braggy benevolent behaviour.
Believe in the Saviour.
But when the truth is lost in their eyes.
Lying might be wise.

Keep dreams stitched to your hem.
So no one can steal them.
And you will never forget.
Where you need to be and where you're at

Always think before you speak.
Never let your secrets leak.
Once the wrong words have been said.
There is a price on your head.

Where normal or strange.
Somethings never change.
And what you swore would never.
Will somehow change forever.

Always give a second chance.
They may have run a foolish dance.
If again they lay off track.
Never look back.

Let experience be a lesson.
Whether you have lost or won.
Victory can quickly turn to defeat.
If you are not firm on your feet.

Remember, Angels always hide their wings.
Devils flaunt their plastic wings.
Beware of the illusion.
When your heart whispers; listen.

16.10.2016

48. Lost & found

To the point of no turning back.
To the point of losing track.
I have gone the uncounting distance.
And where I was.
Was a place of selfish loss.
Lost before, lost I am no more.
Time has the power to create a new hour.
Time; My eternal lover.
Time has rewound.
Lost and found.

How do you know what to find?
Until you know what you have lost.
Almost always we keep looking.
For a missing piece of our heart.
Which is often left, right at the start.
Don't search the world for a key to an open door.
Don't get trapped in trappings.
For 'you' can be found when 'they' are lost.
The walk of liberty starts with the mind.

Liberty, the friend solitude will find.

Something lost can be something found.
Sometimes silence is the loudest sound.
There's a reason why the Earth goes round.
So, we can be lost and found.

16.10.2016

49. Lovers world

Lovers live in their own world.
Oblivious to space and time.
They are in moments of their own making.
A song of their own reason and rhyme.
They may not even notice words said or unsaid.
Happy enough to be in each other's company.
As time itself binds for them.
Looks of love, holding hands, and soul serenity.
The world may look at them.
But the love realized do not care.
All that is precious is the look they give each other.
All they know is that the other is there.
Even these moments are not enough.
As they long to be with the other more.
Stretching time for seconds longer.
As they linger at the leaving door.
Lovers live in their own world.
Oblivious to space and time.
They are in moments of their own making.
A song of their own reason and rhyme.

22.05.2023

50. Meemorphosis

Hey Moon.
I'm a butterfly in her cocoon.
Dreaming dreams & hoping hopes.
Shine your shine on me.
Light me the lane to fly free.
Hey Sun.
I'm a lioness on her run.
Chasing clouds and conquering curiosities.
Ray your ray on me.
Dare me to design my destiny.
Hey Wind.
I'm a hermit by her tree, disciplined.
Praying prays & hymning heals.
Tell your tales to me.
Whisper the way to soul serenity.

Not someone you can program.
I'm ever changing who I am.
One day that & one day this.
It's a miracle meemorphosis.

Hey Time.
I'm a melody making into a rhyme.
Synchronizing spirit & echoing emotion.
Sing your song for me.
Lullaby me to magic and memory.
Hey Universe.
I'm a dot trying to outline my space.
Counting constellations & creating connections.
Glow your glow on me.
Help me define true reality.
Hey God.
I'm a creature who's told she's odd.
Wondering wunders & wishing wills.
Bless your blessings on me.
Grace me to a good eternity.

Not someone you can program.
I'm ever changing who I am.
One day that & one day this.
It's a miracle meemorphosis.

20.10.2016

51. Nocturnal notes

The night is darkness.
The darkness is black.
In this black I see colors.
The colors I want to see.

The world is quietness.
Quietness without loneliness.
Lonesome is the moon.
The moon which is now mine.

I hold a ladder to the sky.
The sky which is so high.
And high are the stars.
The stars that tell stories.

Fairies talk in whispers.
Whispers of the soul.
The soul is holy language.
A language we share.

I see dreams fly with wings.
Wings I wish to have.
To soar through the night.
A night of angels and ghosts.

The night sings to me.
A song that comes to me.
Comes from my lullaby.
A mother's lullaby.

The night is my friend.
A friend who always comes.
Comes to visit me.
Me, who loves the night.

04.10.2016

52. Oh! to be

Oh! to be young.
And have a childish heart.
Feel the whimsy of fun.
Go explore and experiment.
Think of everyday like God's gift sent.
Oh! to be found.
And have a fresh start.
Yet still be like before.
To live free of worry and guilt.
To live free from the chains I've built.
To be popular.
To be confident.
To be charismatic.
To be famous
To be spiritual.
To be divine.
Oh! To be everything you want to be.
And realize your true destiny.
Get the happy ever after
To seek beauty and bliss

And to realize it is this.

30.05.2023

53. Paths & pursuits

Let me wander.
Even if lost.
Let me go...discover.
For every road goes somewhere.
Every road leads somewhere.
Who knows what I'll find.
When my feet catch up with my mind.

And if I'm walking in circles.
At least I would have spun with the earth.
If I'm walking straight with no direction.
Maybe I'll find the end of the world.

In my life.
Its choices.
Let me explore...destiny.
For all rivers flow into the ocean.
All rivers meet at the ocean.
So don't tell me to believe in less.
Of both failure and success.

And if I'm on a wild chase.
At least I would have outrun regret.
If I have travelled far from reality.
Maybe I'm resting with imagination.

And if I go missing.
Maybe I've found the break in time.
And if I never return.
Maybe I am at my destination.

15.10.2016

54. Phantasmagorias

When you close your eyes...
What is it you see?
Your lover? Your ghost? Your God?
A blackness of fleeting images.
Seconds revolving your fragile mind.
Memoryscopic visions of thoughts nearly forgotten.
With eyes closed you are not blind.
So when you open your eyes...
What is it you see?

Do closed eyes reflect recalls of things once seen?
If so, then what can a blind man see?
Does it mean he has no vision?
And sees nothing beyond this darkness?
Or does he see a world so different?
Perceived beyond our perception?
If a blind man can see without sight,
Then it is the mind that sees, not the eyes.

With eyes open...
You can still be blind.
Never sighting what was meant to be.
Luminous roses, swirling wines, stilling blood.
Will then have no distinction.
They are all red.
Your mind is busy, eyes too dim.
You are death walking around undead.
Is there a cure for this blindness?

Asleep or in the waking.
We all see dispelled dreams.
Nothing like before.
Nothing like it might be.
A stretch of possibility.
Just because it lies unseen.
Should it not be believed?
Neither Heaven nor Hell is known by I.
Yet, I have seen it all in my mind's eye.

26.03.2023

55. Prayers

May it be that God's glory has a hand placed on me.
May it be my dreams come true with my destiny.
May it be in life I attain what I am meant to seek.
May it be strength guides me when belief is weak.
May it be I see light in times of obscurity.
May it be in my fall I still hold my dignity.
May it be that I know love, once, before I die.
May it be bliss lies in the wake of tears I cry.
May it be that I perceive the whisper of my soul.
May it be to perfection I play my role.
May it be that I live with no reason for remorse.
May it be I find peace within my heart's doors.
May it be I am not ordinary in whatever I do.
May it be when my task is done, I return to You.

18.10.2016

56. Pulsations

The world is in sacrilege.
History is writing its page.
Broken dreams are building the future.
Apathy has grown into our nature.
Our eyes in fear shrouded.
Our minds in hate clouded.
Mankind is in a race for success.
Taking irremissible decisions.
Making irrevocable changes.
In the name of progress.
Old forsaken for the new.
Not given its respect due.
Development has set a mode to destroy.
Cultures of consumerism.
Vultures of corporations.
It is a profiteer's ploy.
Sacrilege beheld with indifference.
Desensitized by silence.

As the bell of modernization rings.

The seeds we sow in our garden.
Grow into fruits of things we've done.
The choices we make in tranquility.
Lend their power to our loyalty.
The words that we whisper in devotion.
Can cause the shouts of revolution.
Through love we have hope to salvage.
The flight of expressions trapped in a cage.
Tomorrow will flourish from what we today saved.
It will build on how we've now behaved.

For as the bell of modernization tolls.
We have a chance to save our souls -
"Every time we remember preservation;
We retain a part of our civilization."

06.10.2016

57. Purpose

Why are some born wise?
Why are some born into gain?
Why are some born to rise?
Why are some born into pain?

What exactly is time and the best use of it?
What is true love and its kiss?
What is the best way of living – a lot or a bit?
What is the path to bliss?

Does God create everyone equal?
Does the creator have His own hope?
Does the world make us dual?
Does He give us the ability to cope?

Am I the one making my own story?
Am I the one to make a world of us?
Am I the one to defy and define destiny?
Am I the one defining my purpose?

30.5.2023

58. Reason & rapture

I will fall. I will rise.
May live in fool's paradise, but my old soul is wise.
Believe I'm the creator's child. Wonder in my veins.
Flying with friends from different planes.
I will be lost. I will be found.
Curious cats always land on their feet, hitting ground.
I know there is more to life. A cosmic missive.
Designing a destiny we must dare to live.

Been given sunshine for your thunderclouds.
Been given solitary for your crowds.
It's just in a daze of blaze that these feelings dim.
Been given song for your silence.
Been given art for your science.
It's just in a daze of blaze that these feelings dim.
It's just in a daze of blaze that these feelings dim.
Reality-blurring-dreams. Chaos-connecting-clues.
You're my muse. You're my blues.

There are signs.

Signs that surround me – giving me shine.
Telling me all is fine.
Revealing a path that's mine.
Need to awaken and wake the world.
Need to wake and awaken the world.
Need to awaken and wake the world.

06.08.2023

59. Roses

Some roses bloom...
To bring joy to an eye.
Their beauty beholden;
To a passerby.

Some roses bloom...
To be first love's souvenir.
For words fallen shy;
And tongues tied in fear.

Some roses bloom...
To assist a hearts confusion.
When each petal plucked;
Makes closer a decision.

Some roses bloom...
To perfume passions.
It's scent of surrender charms;
A battle without guns.

Some roses bloom...
To be offered in apology.
Fresh blossoms for fresh starts;
Makes forgiveness easy.

But some roses bloom...
To be forsaken on your grave.
As I carry on loving;
A love I could not save.

15.10.2016

60. Seconds

Stand at the edge of a cliff a second away from falling.
Hold my head under water a second too close to
drowning.
I just want to know.
I just want to see.
Is my life full of seconds;
Every breath counted by time.
What if I lost out by a second;
Would this life still be mine?

Think about all the people I wouldn't have met.
If I hadn't been delayed sometimes somewhere.
Would they still have been sent to me someday?
Or did I just find them in a spun second?
Think about how I missed death round the corner.
All those times I decided to walk straight.
Was it meant to be that I would still live?
Or did I change it all with just a second?

Is my life a map by God;

Every second the way He made it?
When I read the map wrong;
Does my road make any difference?
Is my life held by seconds;
A puppet pulled by strings?
What if I choose to make the ending,
Can the seconds still stop me?
Will the seconds still stop me?

19.10.2016

61. Session

Close your eyes and concentrate.
Release your thoughts, meditate
Our minds are in dissection
We are now in session

Believers! What is it you believe?
God. Humanity. Peace prosperity...or immortality?
If you live life like cows led to graze
Do you believe you will receive His grace?
Would you believe in goodness and virtue
If everything you had was taken away from you?
"We all dwell in probability
Your today could be someone's tomorrow
You believe every solution lies in prayer
Yes, he is the creator but is not also the slayer?
Our whole life we are writing a petition
Give us the end, give us salvation
I question not what you believe
Only why you do what you do, my pet peeve.
Maybe you know beyond, more than what I envision

About Enlightenment -sounds like a worthy mission

Disbelievers! What are you so cynical about?
Is it yourself or God you doubt?
Do you not believe in eternal purpose
Or are you runaways from the spiritual fuss?
And what source is it you perpetuate?
For your oscillating existence, if not fate?
"We all have our quiet fears
Wishing them away with sleep, with dreams
But sometimes daylight is harsher than a nightmare.
We are always in preparation
Cloaked and costumed for one performance.
The final curtain falls to echoes of encore."
You disbelieve in the circle
In fairies, ghosts and a Christmas miracle
If everything is just as it seems
Who then, is the spinner of dreams?
Do you have a strong resolution for disbelief
Or did the antagonism come with no relief?

I don't know if there is a God.
I don't know if there is no God.
I believe we are all our own reason
And if He is there, He will have one.

07.10.2016

62. Should my reason rhyme

Should my heart tear,
I'll stitch it back again.
None the worse for wear.

...

Should my wish fly,
I'll ride a paper-plane.
Fetch a star from the sky.

...

Should my mind stray,
I'll find it and explain.
The way to a way.

...

Should my dreams sleep,
I'll count sheep in my brain.
Until awake they can keep.

...

Should my fears arise,
I'll fight them till slain.
Brave and wise.

...

Should my fate turn,
I'll silence complain.
Take a lesson to learn.
...
Should my soul depart,
I'll catch the time train.
End to start.

18.10.2016

63. Sight

Look at the sky.
Don't ask why.
Just look at the sky.
Hear it sigh.
Feel it cry.
As rain...

Look at the moon.
Ask for a boon.
Just look at the moon.
Catch it croon.
Wake up at noon.
As vain...

Look at the flower.
At its best hour.
Just look at the flower.
Feel its power.
Like a lover.
As pain...

Look at the sun.
Not for fun.
Just look at the sun.
Seek the one.
Think if it's done.
As (they) ordain...

Look at the leaf.
For shade relief.
Just look at the leaf.
Is there belief?
Happiness after grief.
As gain...

Sight. Sight. Sight.
Get it right.
With His heavenly might.
Come unto the light.
Sight. Sight. Sight.
Light. Light. Light.
Sight. Sight. Sight.
Might. Might. Might.
Sight. Sight. Sight.

31.05.2017

64. Sisters under the moon

We always understood what each never had to say.
Now we both have to go our own way.
As you walk, hold my heart in you.
And when it beats you will know I'm calling.
Talk to your soul and I will listen.
Afar we may be but we are still one.
Gaze at the sky to see me over here.
As we are sisters.
Sisters under the moon...

We are a part of each other.
We are champions together.
Keep counting time, we will meet soon.
As sisters under the moon...

Idyllic dreams and whimsical stories.
We both created as no one else sees.
Now I pray for them to come true.
Both for me and for you.
Open the door to the unknown.

You won't find yourself alone.
Listen to the rain, know we'll walk again.
As we are sisters.
Sisters under the moon...

We are what they'll never figure.
We hold love that shall linger.
We will be each other's boon.
As sisters under the moon...

Who knew time could fly so fast.
Of all there is, only this shall last.
As we dance in our cocoon.
We are still sisters under the moon.
Sisters under the moon...

20.10.2016

65. Solitude

It may seem rude.
My solitude.
That is all I have.
All I am.
It is my attitude.
My fortitude.
I have nothing I wish for.
Nothing to offer.
Nothing to expect.
Nothing to say.
Nothing to forget.
I have myself to fall back on.

I have nothing to be weak for.
Nothing to hide.
Nothing to fear.
Nothing to feel.
Nothing to lose.
I have myself to live with.
Nothing is wrong.

Nothing is right.
Nothing is far.
Nothing is near.
I am the choice I make.

Please don't question.
My seclusion.
It is not yours.
It is mine.
A divine reparation.
My definition.

09.08.2016

66. Sometimes life

Sometimes life captures you in the most unexpected
ways.
And stays.
There is a beauty in being.
In seeing.
The world through the eyes of a child.
Everything marvellous and not yet mild.
Sometimes don't think with your head first.
Give into your heart's thirst.
And let life capture you in the most unexpected way.
And wait...just wait for it to stay.

27.3.2019

67. Spiritual solarium

They said God would heal me.
From darkness.
From the pain.
And the more I prayed.
The darker I felt.
And the pain?
Well let's just say it stabbed me insane.

They said God would lift me.
So, I lost all of my friends.
So, I would be lost no longer.
And now I have a map.
But have no road.
Where is He?
My arms are open but empty.

They said God gives justice.
So, I tolerated.
In patient faith.
And the more I waited.

The more it became.
And justice?
Is a long due kiss.

My spiritual solarium.
Like a fish in an aquarium.
Sensing a world outside.
Still thinking this is my world.
I waited for a God who didn't come.
I healed me.
Does this mean I am God?

06.06.2015

68. Sun, moon and star

Think twice.
Before you are nice.
Think twice.
Before you try to be wise.
You never know.
Which choice will end up as a show
Sometimes its ok to take it slow.
Figure out your own personality.
Stop dealing with duality.
People may tell you who you are.
And you may forget too.
We all lose once in a while.
We all lose our love for a smile.
But someday eventually.
When you're okay truly.
You'll remember that...
...you also once came from the sun, moon and stars.
Think twice.
And try to be nice.
Think twice.

And try to be a better kind of wise.

5.12.2022

69. Sun sun sunflower

If you've had a bad day.
Here's a sun-flower for you.
For sunflowers always face the light.
So even in your darkest hour.
Of a darkest night.
That no one knows about.
May you find the power.
To lift from self-doubt.
You may fall more than once.
But that's okay.
For in you is the light of a thousand suns.
And one day you will know it.
Glow in it.
Grow in it.
So, if you've had a bad day.
Here's a sun-flower for you.

06.04.2022

70. Thank You

There are tears I cry.
Which make an ocean of love.
Here sails a ship of gratitude.
Which finds light after darkness.
It brings neither treasure nor triumph.
Just a prayer for your happiness...

There are tears I cry.
Which become drops of blissful rain.
Carried on a smiling cloud to a land afar.
They fall with hope to spread cheer.
So that every bad turns good.
And every far turns near...

There are tears I cry.
A tribute for the ones you shouldn't.
Perhaps this isn't enough.
But it is all I can give now.
For all that you have done.
I will forever seal with you −my love...

There are tears I cry.
They are the words I cannot speak.
They fall on your garden of flowers.
So a desert it may never be.
They fill your silences.
So that you may never forget me...

07.09.2016

71. The Avenues

There's a road to that takes you high.
To Heaven & Love.
Been told there's a road to the sky.
So, I always look for it above;
Making maps out of stars.
Talking to the moon.
Chasing the sun ray.
Hoping I'll find the way...soon.

There's a path that God knows.
To Dreams & Paradise.
Been told there's a path that He shows.
For those who wonder wise;
Who dare to take on destiny.
In search of what they seek.
So I try to be my best.
Different from the rest...unique.

There's a chord one can sing.
For Him & Hymn.

Been told there's a chord one can ring.
So I hum to Him;
Hoping to hit the right note.
Rhyming rhythms and soul songs.
With words that dance.
Give me a chance...belongs.

There's a song one can write.
For Prayer & Peace.
Been told there's a song one can rite.
For those who wish release;
To lift into life beyond.
Take your place in the galaxy.
As a star shining bright.
Wishing humans goodknight...eternally.

08.08.2016

72. The bridge

The land of promise was on the other side.
With the river of difficulty flowing beneath.
A brick was laid of ambition.
Another of integrity.
It was cemented with patience.
To build the bridge of opportunity.

People walked on.
Only to be blocked by the pillars of vanity.
Some were afraid to step on.
Overwhelmed by the height of effort.
Others just stood there watching.
The birds of dreams flying high.
And the bridge remained broken...

A few picked up pebbles of greed.
And burdened themselves to slow down.
Many ran halfway back.
When the clouds of doubt grew into a storm.
All of them forgot the path of wisdom.

Distracted by the beauty of ignorance.
And the bridge remained broken...

The land of promise is on the other side.
With the river of difficulty flowing beneath.
The sun of beginning arises.
The wind of time blows.
With changes, the world did change.
All are awoken.
Will the bridge remain broken?
Will the bridge remain broken?
Will the bridge remain broken?

12.08.2016

73. The drifter

I got no plan.
Got no one to be better than.
I follow my time.
Sing to my rhyme.

I want no friend.
Want no people to time spend.
Just want to be lost in the world.
Enjoying every little thing.
Enjoying every little moment.
Maybe pen it in a poem.
Maybe paint it in art.
Maybe capture it in a picture.
Maybe act it out in a me and world movie.
Maybe sing it in a song.

They call me a cheater.
With no responsibility.
They call me a dreamer.
With no possibility.

But I am a drifter.
With my sense own of destiny.

30.5.2023

74. The escapist

At a standstill, I can see my world clear.
Take an honest look at choices that got me here.
Beautiful it's been, wandering the wonder ways.
But do I want to be lost in a maze?

I'm going to have to try to realign.
And make things more than just fine.
Have to find what I truly believe in.
Going to find focus within.
I feel scared. I feel ready.
What does the future hold?
A greater good?
A radiance real?
That will take me beyond...

Like the escapist in running shoes
Chasing distances and rapture realities;
A glow of golden suns; Opening the door to dreams.
Or sharing its keys. #

I'm going to have to try to realign;
And make things more than just fine.
Have to find what I truly believe in.
Going to find focus within.

I escape...
I escape...
I escape...
Unto me.

15.10.2016

75. The freak

When I was born;
I was made whole.
I was flawless;
With a perfect soul.
Just like a rose;
In a crystal vase.
I wish I was close to being clear.
Being dear.

I'm no angel.
Still, I don't belong in hell.
I am only human.
Yet I don't belong here.

I don't care for truth;
That truth which aches.
I live in a dream;
Which truth breaks.
Just like a story;
In your sleep.

I want to be that lie.
More beautiful than truth.

I'm no angel.
Still, I don't belong in hell.
I am only human.
Yet I don't belong here.
I'm no angel.
But I have woven whimsy wings with which
I'll fly...
Fly.
Fly.
Fly.

If it makes you happy,
I'll go away.
But you will miss me.
You will miss me.
For I'm the freak.
I'm the weird one.
Who talks to the moon and the sun.
Who you come to when you have none.
Yes. I am what you seek.
When you want to fly.
When you want to fly.
When you want to fly.

19.10.2016

76. The games I play with God

Before I finish this drink;
Give me a reason not to have another.
Make me a Believer.
Of Goodness, Hope and Fate.
Just grant me the beginning of a wish.
For the rest I will wait.
Give me a reason.
A simple one.
Now the glass I swimming;
I'm not yet done.

If I keep on smiling;
In the face of tragedies.
Will you give out on lease;
(To me) Happiness and Peace?
I will endure all difficulties.
Not asking for it to be easy.
Just lift my spirit.
From time to time.

Now the smile is frozen;
In the face of this mime.

If I leave my shoe;
On the steps of time.
Will true love find me;
At the destined hour?
Those who I love, leave.
Is it not in my power?
Find me an arrow.
Shoot from a bow.
Now I have only You.
For someone to love.

31.05.2016

77. The hangover

Oh ye porcelain gods…
Against all even and odds.
I swear this is the last time I drink.
I feel like I'm the edge of death's brink.
Even my upchucks look like art.
As I can't feel any body part.
Every smell seems immensely stronger.
And the mistakes I've made seem wronger.
My tongue feels like sandpaper.
And my memory is in an abstract blur.
I think I twerked to some trance music.
The mere movement makes me feel sick.
I really didn't mean to send that text.
Do you know what feeling will come next?
Water water I need lots of water.
I look like a scary something in the mirror.
My body craves for some junk food.
And I eat it knowing it will bring no good.
I need sleep sleep and some more sleep.
While my head says things I need to bleep.

This should never ever again occur.
I say till my next hangover.

6.8.2020

78. The moon drives me mad

The moon drives me mad.
Like tides, its happy and sad.
Sometimes it's a creature mystical.
Sometimes it's a mystery maniacal.
Is it the muse of poets?
A keeper of secrets?
Or a setting of a story horror?
A chemical imbalance occur?
It makes the wolves howl.
The creatures of dark growl.
But it also creates love and romance.
A whimsical wonder dance.
Is it a satellite as science describes?
Or a healing as meditation prescribes?
The moon drives me mad.
It brings out in me good and bad.
Sometimes it's a friend for conversation.
Sometimes it's a partner for maddened delusion.

03.01.2021

79. New Poem

79. The need for NO

Most of us spend a lifetime saying yes.
Overstretching ourselves till we're energy less.
We're told it's the best way to be.
The condition of fitting into society.
The good girl.
The polite person.
The do-it-all doer.
Until we become a people pleasing personality blur.

Let it be known.
There is a need for NO.
It's okay to say it.
Its okay to be it.

Define boundaries knowing your worth.
Be self-preserving in pursuing your dreams on earth.
There is a limit to self-sacrifice.
And knowing this is also wise.
The ballsy bitch.
The sometimes selfish.

The restful one.
Take some time in the sun.
Until you are ready to do what has to be done.

Let it be known.
There is a need for NO.
It's okay to say it.
It's okay to be it.

06.04.2022

80. The owners

Some are bright with cheerful a trend.
Almost welcoming like a familiar friend.
Some are melancholic, their shutters drawn.
Shadowing secrets of time bygone.
Some stand solemn, unwarrantedly formidable.
Some awe inspiring, their disposition regal.

Some are prone to experimentation.
Testing spaces unbound by tradition.
Some are olden, beholden with memories.
Wrinkles and flaws, a telling of stories.
Some remain poised in delicate grace.
Some broken-down yet resilience in place.

Houses; each possessing a distinct personality.
Eerily akin to their human's identity.
Do houses take on their occupant's character?
Or do residents grow into their houses' structure?
I wonder if anyone else wonders.
Who really become the owners?

13.10.2016

154

81. The shooting star

Last night I dreamt the perfect dream.
And begged tomorrow not to come.
Then morning awoke.
The silent world spoke.
And my little dream broke...

I hide dreams under my eye lashes.
So no one can see them.
Except for that single tear.
Crystal clear.
Which falls when none are near...

I got to the movies. I visit the old.
And hear of their dreams come true.
I leave feeling fine.
Then come sunshine.
I know those dreams weren't mine...

I take a twinkle, an hour; the colours of a rainbow.
And all the dreams that I know.

And put them in a jar.
The sky is too far.
So I will be my own shooting star...

19.12.2016

82. The silent girl

A piece of sky. In her eye.
A peace of sky. Getting her by.
The stars she cannot see.
But she remembers them from memory.
And there is no moon tonight.
No silver light.

The silent girl sits still.
On her window sill.
And takes in the fill.
Of silence...
The silent girl doesn't cry.
She just heaves a little sigh.
And does ask why.
In reverence...
The silent girl surrenders.
To her dreams, her wonders.
And to her blunders.
In innocence...
The silent girl just breathes.

To the wind in the leaves.
And hopes she receives.
Of penance...

The rays of the day. Is on her way.
The race of the day. Setting what to obey.
The light she cannot stare.
But she braves on to boldly glare.
And find the honour horizon.
Find the One.

The silent girl plots.
Powers her thoughts.
And collects forget-me-nots.
Of remembrance...
The silent girl sews her wings.
Collects her things.
And hymns she sings.
In severance...

She is going to soar.
Settle the score.
She is going to soar.
Open a door.
She is going to rise.
Wake up wise.
She is going to rise.

After she dies.
The silent girl.
Will start to swirl.
Give the world a whirl.
The silent girl.
Will start to swirl.
Give the world a whirl.

Like Jesus.
Like Moses.
Like roses.
Like proses.
Like wunderkind.
Like her inner mind.
Like a onekind.
Like after find.

20.10.2016

83. The test of time

There will be a time;
Where fear precedes you.
There will be a time;
When courage leaves you.
As long as you look into your heart.
There you will find strength.
To walk the path you were meant.
To find your purpose and fulfil it.
Hear no council from another soul.
For it will cloud the wisdom of your own will.

There will be an hour;
Where your character will fall to test.
There will be an hour;
When your faith will fail.
As long as you remember.
That the choice rests in you.
And victory matters;
But is not what counts.
It is the effort and endurance that lives.

You shall find breath to breathe into your life.

What makes for a true hero?
Is it feeling fright yet bellowing bravery?
Is it inner insight or wonder visionary?
Is it in creating or following the line?
Is it a gene that we develop or divine design?
What makes for a true hero...do you know?

30.12.2023

84. The thing with being alone

The thing with being alone.
Is that.
You hear all those thoughts you silenced.
In crowds.
In noises.
In places.
And not all the thoughts are good.
You find it tough to sit with them.
You fidget.
You crave to escape.
The suffocation of silence.
But after a while.
The thing with being alone.
Is that...
You clear all those thoughts you silenced.
In peace.
In submission.
In love.
And...

They become your solace.
The serenity of your silence.

04.06.2022

85. Then & now

When I was a child,
I danced under moonbeams.
Ran through gardens with elves and fairies.
I sat for hours creating stories.
Playing with my friend imagination;
And the ocean;
Was not just sand and sea.
It was mermaids and mystery.

Now, I've grown up;
And if I turn in circles.
Hoping to break free,
They look at me...and say -
"She's a trick.
She is sick."
But really it's just lost magic.

When I was a child,
Little things spellbound me.
Like patterns of shells;

Wishing wells.
Bubble colours caught in the sun.
The wind on my face in a run.
And the fun;
In seek and hide.
In sliding down a slide.

Now, I've grown up;
And if I turn in circles.
Hoping to break free,
They look at me...and say -
"She's a trick.
She is sick."
But really it's just lost magic.

You count coins instead of stars.
You build houses instead of dreams.
For all those 'wise'.
I close my eyes and say –
"I'm not a trick.
I'm not sick...
I'm just finding the lost magic.
I'm just finding the lost magic.
I'm just finding the lost magic."

16.10.2016

86. Things I caught

I shot an arrow into the sky.
To catch a cloud.
And bring it over.
So I could fly.

I stayed awake.
To catch a dream.
And walk the silver thread.
Before it could break.

I stole colours from a butterfly.
To paint my world.
A water colour world.
Hung out to dry.

I went fishing for the moon.
In the waters of an ocean.
And caught drops of it.
On my little spoon.

I caught the sun in a jar.
And kept it hidden.
So the night could stay on.
And I could turn into a star.

I broke the clock on the wall.
To catch time.
So nothing would elude me.
And I could have it all.

06.04.2016

87. Things I love

I love to swing on swings.
The joy that giving brings.
Small and simple things.
And pretending I have wings.

I love wishing wells.
The chime of temple bells.
Anyone who story tells.
And sea side shells.

I love the game of chance.
The power of taking a stance.
The way trees breeze dance.
And words and their nuance.

I love dew drops.
Sea, sand, and flip-flops.
A green field of flowers and crops.
And those moments the whole world stops.

I love the sun at dusk and dawn.
The smell of rain on a fresh lawn.
Chess and the power pawn.
And peace that is found in a day well gone.

I love promises that are meant.
Sweet gifts of smiles sent.
That everyday can bring something different.
And I can live to the fullest this life I've been lent.

12.06.2022

88. Title

I'm bloody good.
I'm bloody bad.
I'm bloody misunderstood.
I'm bloody mad.

I'm bloody brave.
I'm bloody broke.
I bloody well will misbehave.
I'm a bloody joke.

I'm bloody profound.
I'm bloody young.
I bloody won't listen to scold.
I'm bloody stung.

Move my feet to my head.
Bloody steps to a dance town.
And I sway.
In my gleaming gown.

I'm bloody vengeance.
I'm bloody pure.
I'm bloody lost innocence.
I'm bloody sure.

I'm bloody fun.
I'm bloody music.
I'm bloody on the run.
I'm a bloody trick.

I'm bloody free.
I'm bloody null.
I bloody won't be anyone but me.
I'm bloody original.

Move my feet to my head.
Bloody steps to a dance town.
And I sway.
In my gleaming gown.
A queen finding her crown.

12.02.2021

89. Trees

90. Unrealisms

91. Wheel of words

We all have plans for life.
Then life has plans for us.
Where is the communion.
If anytime there was one.

I hear voices.
Saying - make the right choices.
What they tell me to do.
Is not what I want to do.
But then things go bad.
And I feel sad.
If I don't try.
There will always be why.
I've got to go down that road.
Even if it means coming back.
I'm not walking away.
I just need to find my way.
I can never be that gramophone.
Stuck on one track.

When I grow.
I don't want to grow into life.
I want life to grow into me.
I want to write my own story.

15.06.2022

92. Where are you going?

Where are you going?
In such a hurry.
In a world of worry.
Where do you want to go?
That you can't stop admire the flower ground.
Or see the plights of people around.
Or hear the song bird's sound.
Or feel the blessings abound.

Where are you going?
We all have responsibility.
And are answerable to our duty.
But if you fail to see beauty.
In a second's silent serenity.
Where can you go?

Where are you going?
My friend with the frown.
With your world upside down.
Where do you want to go?

Make something of yourself and your name.
To the super high hills of fame.
Is celebrity of cosmosity your aim.
Remember, it is all a life game.

Where are you going?
We all have responsibility.
And are answerable to our duty.
But if you fail to see beauty.
In a second's silent serenity.
Where can you go?

12.06.2022

93. Who am I

Who am I?
A star fallen from the sky?
Who am I?
Do I get to ask why I am here?
Here.
Do I know what it really is?
Am I to believe scientific discoveries?
Am I to believe spiritual theories?
Am I to build on histories?
Am I to learn from memories?

Am I just another human?
Am I my own reflection?
If I'm here now, where was I before?
Why can't I remember anymore?
Do we all come with some purpose?
Or are we all clowns in His circus?
If I am known by what I think;
Then I am only my mind.
If I am known by what I feel;

Then I am only my heart.
But am I just my body in parts?
Or am I what holds it together?
Am I the child of my mother?
A friend, a lover, a sister?
If relations define who I am;
Who then defines my relationships?
Do I get to put together;
The pieces of my character?
Or is it built within my system;
As I go and when I come?
Am I the face I see in the mirror?
Or the voice of the soul I hear?
Am I the breath that keeps me alive?
Am I the will to survive?
Am I a soul waiting to be free?
If a part of God I am,
Where then is He?

Who am I?
A body, a soul, an illusion?
Who am I?
My own or someone else's perception?
Who knows who we are here.
We take our lifetime to discover.
By the time I know the answer.
Would it really matter;

Who I am...here.

24.11.2016

94. Wide eyed antelope

Leaping through the golden fields.
Looking for some poppy seeds.
In a forest not so dense.
A body of innocence.
Full of hope.
There is a wide-eyed antelope.

Happy at home.
This creature had the world to roam.
Bow and arrow, a hunter arrived.
Plaguing the green that thrived.
He wanted green of a different kind.
And no guilt on his mind.
And so it fell to the rope.
The wide-eyed antelope.

You wear him as your skin
Fashion first, no regret within
You eat him out of greed more than necessity
That's why I ask where is the integrity.

If you're going to take, learn to give back.
That's the only way to keep the balance track.

In the way we use the earth and its resources.
In the way we fill our passions and purses.
In the way we create and cope.
Let's always remember the wide-eyed antelope.

30.5.2023

95. Wind voices and other choices

There are voices in the wind.
If we choose to listen.
There are faces in the sky.
If we choose to see.
There are invisible paths.
If we choose to take them.
All of which can take us higher;
To be a wonder-winged flyer...

There is truth in thought.
If we choose to reflect.
There is a lesson to living.
If we choose to learn.
There is wisdom in story words.
If we choose to read right.
All of which can make us lighter;
To be burden free and brighter...

There are holy hands in time.

If we choose to touch it.
There are hopes in our hearts.
If we choose to find it.
There are cosmic codes in the stars.
If we choose to decipher it.
All of which can wake us mightier;
To be our own destiny's writer...

There is energy in everything.
If we choose to feel it.
There is blessed breath in our being.
If we choose to believe it.
There is a glory in God.
If we choose to seek it.
All of which can lead us to the liberator;
And let us be returned to our Creator.

16.10.2016

96. Windows to worlds

Have you ever...?
Opened the door to your dreams.
With a key of inspiration;
And listened to your heart?

Ran away from nothing.
Toward no destination, in no direction.
Just to chase the wind?
Swam in the ocean.
Seeking mermaids and myths.
Held a shell and awaited stories?

Whispered a wish into a tree;
And waited for fairies to reply.
Went searching for belief;
In the forest of faith?
Looked for faces in clouds;
And christened them with names?

Have you ever...?

Borrowed threads from a spider.
To weave a web of wonder;
And catch visions in it?

Got lost in your imagination.
Painting your thoughts;
And wording your silence?
Planted a seed of hope.
For it to reach far and high;
And make a passage to the sky?

Written a letter to God;
And set it sail on the sea.
Sipped on water to taste wine
Or picked pearls in pebbles?
Mistaken coincidence for a miracle
And read a sign in the stars?
Have you ever...?

15.10.2016

97. Wishes

I wish to find the way to be intriguing and impress.
I wish to be a celebrity answering to the press.
I wish to have more so I can help all those who have less.
I wish for light to shine me from this darkness.
I wish for haven's home and destiny's address.
I wish to find the eternal energy from which to harness.

I wish to live my life to the fullest and have fun.
I wish to get the bad things over with and be done.
I wish to have wunderwings and fly to the sun.
I wish to be healthy and do a rising run.
I wish for cupid to find me my truelovingone.

I wish to know realms from beyond that I miss.
I wish to know what existence and this reality is.
I wish to be touched by true love and its kiss.
I wish to know spirituality and its bliss.
I wish to wake up and say my day is this.

I wish to know about the ancient scriptures.

I wish to know about radiance reign raptures.
I wish to be the power that does heart captures.
I wish to know about human and inter-space natures.
I wish to be friends with all kinds of creatures.

I wish to live a long life with my loyal lover.
I wish to blossom like I am a rare flower.
I wish to go on great adventures and discover.
I wish to find the way to will and recover.
I wish to be blessed by every higher power.
I wish to see God before my final hour.

30.5.2023

98. Wistful

Time stretched beyond boundary.
With hours so carefree.
I lay under the sun.
Dreaming dreams and having fun.
The world waiting to be explored.
Left no time to be bored.
Filled with idealism.
I didn't notice my fall.
Into the chasm...
of realism.

Am I the only one,
Who stares at the horizon?
Wondering what's been done,
Of the dreams I'd spun?
Wondering what's become,
Of the dreams I had spun?

Does it reflect in my eyes?
The cost of my sacrifice.

The confines of conformity.
The almost identical identity.
The weight of what I've won,
Has become my secret burden.

Am I the only one,
Who stares at the horizon?
Wondering what's been done,
Of the dreams I'd spun?
Wondering what's become,
Of the dreams I had spun?

12.06.2022

99. Wonderments

I wonder...
Does God ever need sleep?
If mermaids live in the ocean deep.
And I wonder...
How many galaxies are out there?
If every human has a perfect pair.
Sometimes I wonder...wonder what is true.
I do.

I wonder...
What is real and what is not.
How much say we have in fate's plot.
And I wonder...
If wounds ever really time heal?
If secrets buried will surface to reveal?
Sometimes I wonder...wonder what is true.
I do.

I wonder...
Where dreams take us when we sleep.

Why troubles come in a heap.
And I wonder...
If there is a part of the world yet to discover.
Do angels hear the truth of our prayer?
Sometimes I wonder...wonder what is true.
I do.

I wonder...
If the universe is made of music.
Can we heal the old and sick.
And I wonder...
If wishes come true on a shooting star.
Is there a way to peace in war.
Sometimes I wonder...wonder what is true.
I do.

I wonder...
Of things strange and new.
Like who painted the horizon hue.
And I wonder...
Where the time of today goes?
How to find happiness in all our woes.
Sometimes I wonder...wonder what is true.
I do.

I wonder...
If souls realize enough to remember.

How things happen as they do occur.
And I wonder...
Who created us to be so as we are?
How many miles is it to Heaven so far.
Sometimes I wonder...wonder what is true.
Wonder I do.
For me and you.
I do.
Until I go blue.
Wonder I do.
For me and you.
I do.

19.10.2016

100. Woven Woman

Who says I don't have innocence?
I don't let it show because people taught me to think
twice.
Unless I trust you, I deal with instinct and sense.
As I learnt that I don't always have to be nice.
Why are women expected to be subservient?
Why are we not told about our goddess form?
Why do we always get judgement?
Why do we have to follow the norm?
#I'd rather be a rightful rule breaker.
Baring my cosmic claws.
I'd rather be a wunder waker.
Accepting all my flaws.#

Who said I don't have a soft heart?
I just protect it with an armour shield.
Before being hurt, I like to play it smart.
When you're worth the love, I yield.
Why are women not taught about their inner power?
Why do women always have to bend?

Why not be both the petals and thorns of a flower?
Why won't the conformity end?
#I'd rather be a rightful rule breaker.
Baring my cosmic claws.
I'd rather be a wunder waker.
Accepting all my flaws.#

Be a woman bold and brave.
Don't be a system slave.
Sometimes have fun and misbehave.
Live up fully the life God to you gave.

12.02.2021

9 789369 530700